If you only knew

Beatrice Alys

BookLeaf Publishing

Presentation by *BookLeaf Publishing*

Web: www.bookleafpub.com

E-mail: info@bookleafpub.com

ISBN: 9789357445122

First edition 2021

DEDICATION

Alhamdulillah.

For the one who I love with all my heart,

and for all those who walk with me on this path.

Thank you.

ACKNOWLEDGEMENT

Alhamdulillah Rabbul Alameen:
All praise is to the Lord of all the Worlds.

PREFACE

Bismillahir Rahmanir Rahim:
In the name of God, Most Gracious, Most Merciful.

WARNING

This body runs on extreme temperatures:

A corpse in a steaming bath,
a beating heart in an ice box.

Handle with caution.

I don't want to write poetry

I don't want to write poetry
like Catholic schoolchildren in uniform
or tulips in straight rows.

I want to write poetry

like 7 years old in a mud puddle
and dandelions growing beside the concrete on
the way to school.

A weed is a flower nobody planted,
but still, I like their colour
and I like to blow and pretend I'm making
wishes
like a kid who doesn't care,

because a flower is a flower,
no matter where it grows.

Home

When I was innocent,

stealing into my mother's bed
at midnight,
I learnt
there is a veil that separates
love and loneliness -

a distance like
a dark hallway,
and that a warm embrace
contains emptiness,

both safe and suffocating.
The difference
between four walls
and a prison

is a locked door.

that Black Dog

Once upon a time, it was only a puppy.

It found me in my rage, cloaked in resentment,
wet with a storm of tears and trembling with the
thunder of frustration.
Dog, I thought, noticing it for the first time.
Looked, but did not touch.
It sat at the foot of my bed and watched me.

When I moved, it trotted some distance away.
Most days I forgot it was there. It made no noise
–
a mark of its breed.
The other creatures that came and clawed and
scratched,
they were violent, visible, mean.
But it didn't even bark.

Too young to care, too busy to notice.
Until one day, it moved closer, a fraction of an
inch.
The clamour of the world around me had
muffled its approach
and before I knew it,
it was close enough to see,

just outside the periphery.

Hello, I thought, perplexed.
I didn't recognize its form,
so much bigger was it now, halfway to grown.
There was something in its eyes,
a predator's stillness. If it could move its lips
into a grin,
it would have been wolfish.
But still, it didn't speak.

I began to wonder why it followed me, and more
importantly,
Why haven't I noticed it before?
It offered no answers, just kept trotting at my
side,
patient.

While I still could, I shrugged it off.
Soon enough, its cousins –
the hyena and the vulture –
began to pay me visits.

At first I hated them, the hyena in particular –
it gave me no respite, striking at will,
cackling in delight.

The vulture was kinder,
wrapping me up in its downy feathers

and hissing softly in my ear,
a sweet-mouthed liar licking wounds and
whispering away my fear.

The years passed, and no sound from the hound,
who by now was full-size, almost to my chest,
huge and dark as a moonless sky.

Its silence had numbed me,
lulled to blindness, unaware of the monster in
my mind.

That's what almost killed me.

It didn't give me a chance to react –
bared its teeth, charged full-throttle,
not an ounce held back.
It would be an understatement to say I was
caught off-guard.
I fell backwards soundlessly
and it opened up a chasm,
an abyss that cracked the earth
and splintered my beloved home,
that place of strength that I'd once called my
own
it tore limb for limb as it yielded, soft and
supple, unprepared.
I could only gaze impassive as it devoured
everything I'd cherished,

until I no longer cared.

In the aftermath, I wandered alone through the wreckage.
I sat amidst the rubble, playing with the glass.
It trotted over,
almost guiltily,
and lay its head in my lap.
I looked down into its eyes,
fathomless, large and black,
and realised I loved it back.

Now it sleeps beside me,
and enveloped in its warmth,
I wipe my tears with its fur
and while away the days,
stroking it for hours.

We have our problems of course,
nothing that we can’t resolve -
except for one dilemma.

It has an appetite for meat,
and though I give my flesh wholeheartedly
my pet will have nothing left to eat.

6:30pm in the kitchen

I'm preparing a meal,
holding the knife carefully,
chopping onions, garlic,

tossing my feelings into a pan.

I wonder if he'll taste the anger in this.

The bitter resentment,
the tang of contempt,
an entire tablespoon of frustration.

I turn the heat up,
stir,
let them dissolve.

It's bubbling.
Turn the heat down.

I check for the smell of frayed nerves,
not too bad.
A punch of salt -

I use my own -

I'm done.
I call him to the table,
Watch expectant as he takes a mouthful -
he's quiet for a second. Then:
"Mm, wow, it's so good."
Hmm.
Bon appétit, I guess.

Tell me, is it a fire?
Or

I smell smoke.
See it coming from my left,

Helpless as it lays its hands
Around my neck
Then, the heat
Eating into me like poison red.

Curling into foetal position,
Opening doors best left closed.
Letting the air over this bed grow choking,
Drowning myself in the silence. Hello? Are you
still there
?

Leave me

Leave me here
to dance with isolation,
let it spin me dizzy
until I fall asleep.

Leave me here
while I make a home
out of my prison,
dress it up with pillows.

Leave me here
so I lose track of time
while the river goes on running
and my friends become goodbyes.

Leave me here
so my bones grow hollow
and my body sinks into the mattress
and my soul sticks to the ceiling.

Leave me here
when my thoughts become an oil spill
and my goodwill dies of starvation
and all the fish are poisoned.

Leave me here
until all I know of living
is memories of feeling, resurrected
in my dreams and nightmares.

Leave me here
and never ask yourself
if you should have stayed.

Injustice

100 shots fired,
99 cold blooded
one in self defence.
But the trial
led by reptiles
isn't making any sense -
it's equating
99 mouths, a chorus
with just one voice.

The truth is louder
than blows and blood,
the truth
will wring the life out of falsehood
will kill it where it stood.

The result is
nothing.
Silence that echoes
in the books,
let there be truth
in the pictures,
in the ruins of an empire
built on soot.

A panther, dark as night
prowls down the street.
The jungle tears its hide
but does not leave scars,
the black cat bleeds
on the concrete,
and from its wounds
grow roses sweet.

Death is a jacket

Death is a jacket
tied around my waist
now the girl who gave it to me
is six feet under.

Death is her Facebook page,
buzzing with life
now that the truth is out.
They put her in a box,
but she only smiles.

Death is a memory,
New York during a hurricane -
they thought we'd be risking our lives,
Times Square empty like the threat
in our minds.

Death is anger,
wondering why the news was silenced
when it's no secret
that there are no prisoners
in its mortal crusade.

Death is a promise
I make to her with my time,

wishing I could explain
how I loved her,
but I don’t miss her yet.

Roses

You told me
you didn’t cry at your mother’s funeral
or for a long time after.
You saved the sorrow
in an empty glass inside

until, you told me,
it was a bouquet of roses
a woman lay on her husband’s grave
that made the water overflow,
spilling repentant from your eyes.

Now it’s your funeral,
your grave Grandma brings the roses to.
I stare silent at the flowers,
ashamed to tell you
that I feel the same.

Age

Oh tree,
why are you so bare?

Did you forget your clothes somewhere
in Autumn?

You're barely there,
an echo of winter
against her song of summer.

Your bony fingers curl,
all stiff joints bent with a vengeance,
twisted and starving —

look at those plump clusters,
green limbs of fresh young flesh
swaying in the wind,
dense with the collected rain.

A pregnant thunderstorm came
and gave birth to new life,
suckled it with water.

It swallowed thickly, grew heavy,
arms reaching for the floor.

But yours soar, scratch the sky,
crooked, defiant.

You spat it out,
kept only a little in your mouth,
not enough for a single bud to sprout.

Suit yourself -
no doubt you've had all winter
to figure this one out.

It's good to see that you're still standing.

It's a reminder
that Death doesn't die by seasons,
but lives in the silence,
standing
still.

Rest

I crave
a sunny room
and a cup of tea,
the moon
splashing through the window,
carving up the floor,
stars in the darkness
roaring bright and ageless,
whispering their secrets to me
in the silence of other people's sleep.

They have taught me the difference
between peace and quiet.

In that space
I wonder,
if time were real
would it laugh?
Or would it stand still,
balancing the end
on one finger
and the beginning
on its toes.

I guess I'll never know.

My friend

I contemplate you
quietly,
taking care
to act nonchalant while I do.

The Love
that fills this silence
is still
the best I've ever known.
It was with years
of joy and water,
sun and tears,
nurtured and like a sapling grown
into a wild, flowered, timeless thing
entirely my own.

I will dissolve

It’s five sixteen on a Sunday and the sun’s still up.

My heart feels cracked,
pores of a desert floor open-mouthed begging
for water, relief.
No rain, no calm
so my chest keeps shaking.
My stomach feels broken, breaking,
suffocated and imploding under the weight
of this electric fear that hooked its claws into my veins
and jitters them wildly, playing me like a violin.
No music but silence. My own
silence from a closed mouth and a trembling lower lip
and the water rising, hovering over the edge
but then retreating back inside.
We don’t want to waste,
we don’t want to admit there's a drought
that the child, long buried
might still try to shout,
calling from beneath this trembling stone called a body.

Sometimes I want to cut open my marrow,
take a knife from my chest all the way down
and flesh around inside for the hard bits,
the shards of granite
cutting up my intestines, blocking my air,
the bolus of hair that's been clogging my system
since time immemorial, won't let me
decompose.

I suppose I miss my bruises when they're gone,
because I love the way their colour makes the
suffering like art,
uses shades of pain to illustrate
so I become a gallery and everyone around me
becomes a witness.

I like to believe my back is breaking like Atlas
and that one day,
if not in Death then maybe in a miracle,
that weight will lift
and I will feel my muscles crease like paper
unfolding -
only then, light and unburdened, I will flutter
away,
like a scribble pencilled into the jaw of eternity
and into its blackness I will dissolve.

Before I go

Give me
the hot August sky
that sweats buckets into the ocean,
that spills rivers
into the mouth of parched land,
grows roots
in vacant parking lots
where the earth's choked breath comes gasping,
as from her mouth spring saplings
that will not make it to autumn.

Give me
the snow that whispers silence on crowded streets,
embraces every leaf and waste bag that greets her,
dances in her sparkling dress for the sun
until his gaze melts her
and the world is pregnant with spring.

Give me
the blossoming -
a touch of peach on her fresh apple cheeks
as she watches the young shoots stretch,
their stems and petals heavy with pollen,

emblazoning the wind with their scent
as they do, the bees and the birds
growing wild with thirst.
And when summer's child is full grown,
tall and green with life
and swimming with the wind in the grass
through the fever of days
stretching like cats,

Give me
the phoenix
whose colours envelop the canopies,
singing the swan song of red
before waltzing adrift on a sigh
until the sky echoes the cry before dark.

And when the ritual stars come smiling,
cackling, jostling for space,
shouting across years to be heard
and telling the stories of the minutes on earth,
as the moon patiently bids them goodbye,
before I go,
give me dawn.

Mother, I found God

Mother,
I found God.

I know
your reservations -
I was raised beside them,
your prejudice and fears as familiar
as the taste of your food.

I beg you,
don't frown when I tuck my hair away,
this cloth a barrier from eyes
like the sheets you'd tuck me into,
your softness
shielding me from the night's cruel embrace.

Look
past the early mornings, stolen prayers
and a language
you've only ever heard on the lips of an enemy
or a stranger.

Listen for the sound
of my eager heart
whispering behind closed doors.

Watch
as I empty myself
for the life of a full moon,
seeking only to drink the light
of the One who fills the sky with it.

Consider
your own soul,
gentle as the words you use to greet the world
opening like the petals in spring
to the love of He who filled your body and your heart
with me.

Mother, I found God.
I pray you find Him too.

Clouds

Somewhere above the clouds
I look up
and wonder how, looking down
is the One who made it all,
watching me.

If we fall
from this height,
where you can see the skyscraper toothpick
heads
we would fall like a tumble
out of bed on a Monday,
we would hit the ground
lighter than feathers,
storming like a hurricane.

Would it hurt,
our bodies violently reunited
with the Earth from which we came?
Little matter, really
but I wonder what my soul would see
when it leaves its cage,
when it's finally free,
soaring dizzyingly
back to its Lord,

awaiting His Word.

A thunder clap,
and we all fall,
level playing field for all.
Who can knock on God's door
on the day the illusion is no more?
Who can ask permission
to move mountains
like when we had time
taking free real estate of our minds,
making us believe
we had today, tomorrow,
the day before. It happened,
we walked the Earth in shadow,
we led the blind in darkness.

Only by our Lord's permission
do we see -
there is no Light without Him,
there is no better way to be.

The time

Lend me an eager ear,
my dear,
it's time you knew about the end:

The day the sun
no longer rises from the East
we won't be able to pretend.

Open your eyes,
before it's over
this vast illusion, loud and sweet

the earth runs dry,
gold bright and blinding
will promise their defeat.

The great deceiver,
know his tricks,
recite the words that we know well.

Our Book protects us
when he promises
a paradise that leads to hell.

The Beast will speak,
the war will rage,
and the time draws ever near -

but hold fast
to the truth, to our beloved
and the only One we fear.

Inheritance

My father gave me
wide eyes, scrutinizing.
My mother gave me
gentle hands, forgiving.

My brother taught me
patience, a watchful gaze
greener with keenness

than my own misty ocean blue -
my little seedling, now I wonder
what will I pass on to you?

Will it be your grandma's will,
iron that would split a rock in two?
Maybe your grandfather's nose,
or his knowledge, tried and true?

Or will you be your father's equal,
his pride, his smile,
will you be moulded in his shape?
I wonder at the form you'll take

a book whose cover I'll know well,
your flesh bound within my womb

I anticipate your voice, your sound,
your smell.
But no matter what you look like
or if you come at all,
I pray

your soul responds
in eagerness and baby steps
to the prayer
when it calls -
to peace, to surrender,
to communion with the One
who owns it all.

My true inheritance is this, my love,
a simple phrase to learn:
Inna lillahi wa inna ilayhi raji'oon -
From Him we come
and to Him we shall return.

93:5 - And your Lord will give you, and you will be pleased

From the beginning
you were the one
I thought I was waiting for,
the one who made all that time seem like

dandelion fluff in the wind.
I was counting daisy petals
for days on end,

wishing, wondering
if you were out there.
In my childish dreams
you were the one who saved me,

who would take me far away.
Who knew that
one day,
I'd fly an ocean

just to make a promise.

To you,
and the One who truly saved me,
who gave me this love
as a promise and a reminder

of what forever looks like
on a dying world.
I wish I could tell her,
that daydreaming girl
what awaited her.

I don't know what the future holds,
but what I know now that I didn't back then:
if I hold on
to this promise, and your hand
we'll be at peace from now
until the end.

The ocean

I’m a little girl on a sailboat,
and I’m watching dawn sparkle on the water.

I’m musing on the fathomless depths below.

I’m thinking
how there is so much darkness,
so much silence.

Creatures known and unknown,
beautiful and terrifying.

It spans continents,
it hosts mountains.

It is cold and warm,
calm and destructive,
clear and murky.

It is both, and all,
at once.

But I’m still a little girl on a sailboat,
looking at the sky,
asking my Lord where I’m going,

and why.

He is right there with me, my Guide.
He reassures me
there's a reason the horizon line is never still,

that there is no errant shore,
nowhere I could be so lost
that I could lose His embrace.

He is all-encompassing,
His Grace is vaster than my hopes,
soaring above the clouds,
or sinking deep below the waves.

He gives me a ship,
He blows wind in my sails,
He teaches me to row, to read the stars
and to weather every storm.

He is the calm, the Peace,
that I yearn for with every living cell.
Drawing every breath,
He is what my heart longed to find
when I was blind with seeing eyes.

A breathing corpse,
slowly losing blood.
The salt water still burns my wounds

but the pain is a sign I'm healing,
a sign that I'm alive.

I'm still swimming upstream,
true,
but sometimes I'll float downstream too.
And when I'm back in open water,

I remember hope
is flowing from my heart
faster than I can think.

My head could never compete,
so I try and surrender it
back to the sea,
cast it overboard.

And it anchors me,
I smile, and I set sail.

www.ingramcontent.com/pod-product-compliance
Lightning Source LLC
Chambersburg PA
CBHW051744130826
49812CB00033B/998
9789357445122